THE
WAR OF 1812

The War of 1812

BY KATIE MARSICO

Content Consultant
John W. Hall
Ambrose-Hesseltine assistant professor of U.S. military history
University of Wisconsin–Madison

ABDO
Publishing Company

CREDITS

Published by ABDO Publishing Company, 8000 West 78th Street, Edina, Minnesota 55439. Copyright © 2011 by Abdo Consulting Group, Inc. International copyrights reserved in all countries. No part of this book may be reproduced in any form without written permission from the publisher. The Essential Library™ is a trademark and logo of ABDO Publishing Company.

Printed in the United States of America,
North Mankato, Minnesota
062010
092010

♻ THIS BOOK CONTAINS AT LEAST 10% RECYCLED MATERIALS.

Editor: Amy Van Zee
Copy Editor: Susan Freese
Interior Design and Production: Christa Schneider
Cover Design: Christa Schneider

Library of Congress Cataloging-in-Publication Data
Marsico, Katie, 1980-
   The War of 1812 / Katie Marsico.
      p. cm.
   Includes bibliographical references and index.
   ISBN 978-1-61613-688-8
   1. United States—History—War of 1812—Juvenile literature. I.
   Title.
   E354.M273 2010
   973.5'2—dc22

                                    2010013518

The War of 1812

TABLE OF CONTENTS

Francis Scott Key's handwritten draft of what would eventually become the lyrics to "The Star-Spangled Banner"

The Flag
That Waved On

On the morning of September 14, 1814, U.S. author and lawyer Francis Scott Key looked anxiously over the waters of Baltimore Harbor off the coast of Maryland. He was desperate to catch a glimpse of Fort McHenry, which guarded the entrance to the harbor. For the past 25 hours, British forces stationed in nearby Chesapeake Bay had been attacking the fort. They had been using rockets and powerful guns called mortars, which were capable of firing shells at great heights within close range.

The battle marked more than two years of fighting between the United States and Great Britain. Although the War of 1812 (1812–1815) officially began in June 1812, it involved issues dating back to the American Revolution (1775–1783). Fighting between the two nations was fierce, and it was not always clear who had the advantage. Just one month before the attack on Fort McHenry, the British had invaded Washington DC. They had burned down the White House and several other government buildings. Now, the British hoped to overtake Baltimore as well.

Defining a Nation

When it declared war on Great Britain in 1812, the United States was still a rather young nation compared to many nations in Europe. The United States was not quite 36 years old at the time. In discussing the War of 1812, one French diplomat remarked, "War has given the Americans what they so essentially lacked—a national character."[1] Today, most agree that the war helped define the United States as an independent nation that would not easily be conquered.

*A depiction of British forces attacking Fort McHenry
on September 13, 1814*

Before the attack had started, Key and U.S.
Colonel John Stuart Skinner had approached British
commanders aboard a ship in Chesapeake Bay, the
HMS *Tonnant*. Their goal was to obtain the release
of one of Key's friends, whom the British had
imprisoned. The pair was successful in persuading

enemy officials to let this man go. However, they were not permitted to return to Baltimore Harbor immediately.

The British were on the verge of launching their attack on Fort McHenry. They were afraid that if they released Key and Skinner, the two would report Britain's position and plans to the U.S. military. As a result, the men were escorted back to their own ship, where they were kept under guard during the 25-hour battle. Throughout the night, gunfire broke the silence and rockets lit up the dark sky. As the men waited, they struggled to determine if Baltimore had fallen to Great Britain.

When dawn finally came, Key was deeply moved by the sight of the U.S. flag still flying proudly over the fort. He was so moved that he wrote a poem about what he saw called "The Defence of Fort McHenry." Today, the words of Key's poem are

Deserving a Song

After Key wrote his poem "The Defence of Fort McHenry," he explained exactly what about the attack on the fort inspired him to write the poem. In describing the moment he spotted the U.S. flag still waving, he said, "Then, in that hour of deliverance, my heart spoke. Does not such a country, and such defenders of their country, deserve a song?"[2]

better known as the lyrics to "The Star-Spangled Banner," the United States' national anthem:

> *O say can you see, by the dawn's early light, / What so proudly we hail'd at the twilight's last gleaming? / Whose broad stripes and bright stars, through the perilous fight, / O'er the ramparts we watch'd, were so gallantly streaming? / And the rocket's red glare, the bombs bursting in air, / Gave proof through the night that our flag was still there. / O say, does that star-spangled banner yet wave / O'er the land of the free and the home of the brave?[3]*

Centuries after Key wrote down his thoughts about the attack on Fort McHenry, the U.S. flag continues to symbolize the freedoms for which so many citizens sacrificed their lives during the War of 1812.

Great Britain and the United States went to war for several reasons, and both nations experienced

The National Anthem

The U.S. government officially adopted "The Star-Spangled Banner" as the country's national anthem in 1931. During World War II, which was fought from 1939 to 1945, many people played the song before sporting events to encourage a sense of patriotism and endurance. That tradition is still followed today.

triumphs and defeats. Historians still debate which side, if any, actually won the war. Yet, some points cannot be disputed, including the fact that after the war, the United States had a feeling of renewed independence from Great Britain, which had controlled it just decades prior.

A SECOND FIGHT FOR FREEDOM

The War of 1812 was fought over several controversial issues. One issue was Great Britain's efforts to restrict trade between the United States and other countries in Europe. A second issue was that British naval commanders were forcing U.S.

The Brick Star That Stands Guard over Baltimore

Fort McHenry dates back to the era of the Revolutionary War. The colonists were worried that British forces would attempt to attack Baltimore, so they quickly constructed a series of earthen mounds on Whetstone Peninsula in Chesapeake Bay. A peninsula, which is a strip of land surrounded by water on three sides, was clearly an ideal location for a guard post. Also, the Whetstone Peninsula was far enough from Baltimore to protect the city from any real danger. Enemy vessels had no choice but to sail past the peninsula if they wanted to enter Baltimore Harbor.

The British never attacked Baltimore during the Revolutionary War, but the Americans continued to build up Fort McHenry all the same. By the time fighting broke out between the United States and Great Britain in 1812, a brick fort had been constructed in the shape of a five-pointed star. A few soldiers were positioned at each point, where they had an excellent view of the points on either side of them. The fort's shape also allowed troops to guard all the surrounding land effectively.

In 1783, the British controlled much of Canada.

seamen into their service. A third issue was Great
Britain's supposed role in encouraging Native
Americans to raid frontier settlements. Critics
argued that going to war with Great Britain was
simply an excuse for President James Madison to
expand U.S. borders south as well as north into

British-controlled Canada. Citizens who supported the war insisted it was necessary for the United States to establish its freedom from Great Britain once and for all.

Great Britain had controlled the American colonies until 1776, when colonial leaders officially declared their independence. In 1775, they began fighting the Revolutionary War to win their freedom. By 1783, American patriots had succeeded in this goal. It was clear, however, that the British resented losing the American colonies. They were determined to hold onto their territories to the north and northwest in Canada.

Yet, as the years passed, Great Britain also became involved in conflicts in Europe. The British fought in the French Revolution (1789–1799) and the Napoleonic Wars (1803–1815). While the British fought France for control over Europe, the United States attempted to remain neutral. Over time, though, this became increasingly difficult. European ships started seizing U.S. vessels, and Great Britain began forcing U.S. sailors into its service. By the summer of 1812, President Madison was eagerly asking Congress for a formal declaration of war on Great Britain.

Madison got his wish, and the United States went to war with Great Britain. Over the next two and a half years, fighting took place in locations ranging from the Great Lakes of North America to islands off the northwest coast of Africa. When the fighting finally stopped, people from all walks of life, from Native Americans and Louisiana pirates to future U.S. presidents and British naval heroes, were able to claim they had played a role in the war. And after the last shot was fired in 1815, one of the few clear outcomes was that the United States was indeed free from Great Britain.

James Madison was the fourth president
of the United States.

A busy Philadelphia, Pennsylvania, street in 1800

THE ROAD TO WAR

The early 1800s was an exciting time for the newly founded United States. Americans eagerly set up businesses and homesteaded farms in the Northeast, and pioneers explored and settled areas along the nation's southern and western frontiers. The country seemed filled with a spirit of freedom and opportunity.

Yet, this was also a time of uncertainty and fear. As the nation expanded, Native Americans who were forced off their lands sometimes led raids on frontier settlements. Both pioneers and native people died as a result of this fighting. The situation was made worse by the fact that the British, who controlled much of Canada, supported and encouraged the Native Americans. The British presence in Canada worried most U.S. citizens. With British support, it seemed the raids would continue.

During the 1780s, the United States claimed the land that became known as the Northwest Territory. It included the area northwest of the Ohio River, including parts of what are now the states of Ohio, Indiana, Illinois, Michigan, Wisconsin, and Minnesota. Much of this territory touched the Great Lakes, so it was not far from Canada.

Although Great Britain hoped to limit expansion of the United States, it was more concerned with developments closer to home. The French Revolution and the Napoleonic Wars forced the British to devote much of their military attention to fighting France for control of Europe.

The United States tried to remain neutral in the overseas conflict, but neither Great Britain nor France made doing so easy.

Both countries began forming naval blockades to prevent the enemy from receiving food and other supplies. The blockades also hurt U.S. merchants, who had hoped to continue trade with both countries despite their being at war. President Thomas Jefferson responded to the European blockades by encouraging Congress to pass the Embargo Act of 1807, which essentially prohibited trade with most of Europe. Jefferson believed this legislation would punish the French and the British and teach them to be more respectful of U.S. ships. Unfortunately, the Embargo Act had little effect on the two European powers and it damaged U.S. businesses a great deal. In 1809, trade was reopened, except with Great Britain and France.

The Embargo Act's Effect on Trade

U.S. trade suffered greatly as a result of the Embargo Act. In 1807, U.S. merchants earned approximately $108 million by selling goods abroad. By the next year, however, those earnings had been reduced to just $22 million.

A Deadly Example of British Impressments

The fighting overseas had other negative effects on the United States.

The British began to impress U.S. sailors, or force them into British naval service. Great Britain claimed it was justified in doing this—it was merely taking back British subjects who had boarded U.S. ships to avoid performing their duties in the Royal Navy.

Tensions over this issue reached a fever pitch in the summer of 1807. On June 22, U.S. sailors stationed on the USS *Chesapeake* left port in Virginia completely unaware they would soon be overtaken by the HMS *Leopard*, a British vessel. The U.S. sailors were not far from their own coastline when they saw the *Leopard* approach. The commander of the British ship ordered Commodore James Barron, the commander of the *Chesapeake*, to allow members of the British crew to board. He believed four British subjects were hiding on the U.S. ship.

Barron refused to allow the British crew to board the *Chesapeake*, so the British opened fire. Historians believe three U.S. sailors were killed during the clash and another 18 were wounded, including Barron. The U.S. crew quickly lowered their flag to indicate surrender, and members of the Royal Navy climbed aboard. They took four sailors from the *Chesapeake* and imprisoned them. In the end,

Officers aboard the USS Chesapeake *surrendered to the British HMS* Leopard.

only one sailor turned out to be a British subject. Two others were U.S. citizens who had voluntarily enlisted in the Royal Navy and then deserted.

Americans were used to hearing news of the British impressing U.S. sailors. However, they were outraged to learn the *Leopard* had attacked the *Chesapeake* and taken American lives. President Jefferson angrily instructed British warships to steer clear of U.S. waters. He also declared the British should pay reparations, or financial compensation, for the killings and injuries. Great Britain eventually gave in to Jefferson's demands. However, it would take four years for both nations to agree on specific terms of repayment.

In the meantime, Americans did not hesitate to express their fury. One writer for the *Washington Federalist* wrote on July 3, 1807,

> We have never, on any occasion, witnessed the spirit of the people excited to so great a degree of indignation, or such a thirst for revenge, as on hearing of the late unexampled outrage on the Chesapeake. *All parties, ranks, and professions were unanimous in their detestation of the . . . deed, and all cried aloud for vengeance.*[1]

ISSUES INVOLVING NATIVE AMERICANS

Over time, tensions increased over British impressments, poor

Surrender

In addition to angering many Americans, the fight between the USS *Chesapeake* and the HMS *Leopard* also stirred widespread uncertainty. The U.S. ship had surrendered quickly because it was ill prepared to fight. Even so, people wondered if this event indicated how the United States would stand up to Great Britain in a naval war. Officials of the U.S. military held Commodore Barron responsible for giving in to the enemy so hastily. He was court-martialed and banned from serving in the navy for the next five years.

trade relations with Europe, and the constant threat of Native American raids supported by Great Britain. By 1811, most U.S. citizens and politicians were thinking about war. And just as Americans' attitudes toward the British worsened, so did their already strained relationship with local Native Americans.

Many tribal leaders resented being pushed off their lands as the United States expanded. This included brothers Tecumseh and Tenskwatawa, who were Shawnees. Like many other Native Americans, they were tired of treaties with the white settlers being broken or changed. Many tribal leaders watched their people lose their homes, hunting grounds, and ways of life.

This growing frustration led to confrontations such as the Battle of Tippecanoe in the fall of 1811. At the time, William Henry Harrison was governor of the Indiana Territory. He discovered Tecumseh and Tenskwatawa were encouraging many tribes east of the Mississippi River to fight the white settlement of the area. The Shawnee brothers lived in a town known as Tippecanoe, just north of present-day Lafayette, Indiana. To prevent a possible rebellion by the tribes, Harrison ordered approximately

1,100 U.S. troops to that area. Though Tecumseh was away at the time, Tenskwatawa urged his followers to attack the troops. The two-hour Battle of Tippecanoe, which occurred on November 7, 1811, resulted in the Native Americans' defeat. However, 37 U.S. soldiers died in the battle, and more than 100 were wounded.

While U.S. forces won the battle, their feelings of victory were mingled with fear and anger. A number of leaders in Washington DC believed the British had encouraged

Influential Shawnee Siblings

Shawnee leader Tecumseh was born in 1768 in what is now the state of Ohio. He quickly earned a reputation for being a fearless warrior who resented white settlers pushing into Native American territory. Tecumseh realized one tribe alone could not overcome the growing number of pioneers. He urged many tribes to unite against a common enemy: the United States. Tecumseh also encouraged his people to fight alongside the British during the War of 1812. He hoped Great Britain would help preserve Native American lands if it won the war.

Tecumseh never lived to see these ambitions realized. He was killed during a battle in Canada in 1813. After his death, many tribes lost their sense of unity in resisting U.S. expansion.

Tenskwatawa, who was born in 1775, did not have great physical strength or military skills, but his people gradually accepted him as a powerful prophet. They were inspired by his promise that native power would be restored by resisting white influence and culture.

Unfortunately, the Shawnees' faith was shaken when Tenskwatawa told them bullets fired by U.S. soldiers during the Battle of Tippecanoe would not harm them. After about 40 Native Americans lost their lives that day, survivors had far less trust in their prophet. By the time Tenskwatawa died in 1836, he was not as respected as he had been during the War of 1812.

the Shawnees to fight. After Tippecanoe, these leaders became more convinced than ever that Great Britain's presence in Canada posed a serious threat to U.S. settlement of the western Great Lakes. In the months that followed, the leaders would use this argument as another reason for the United States to declare war on Great Britain. The British were clearly standing in the way of the United States' ability to grow as an independent nation.

U.S. soldiers were victorious over the Shawnee in the
Battle of Tippecanoe.

Henry Clay was a prominent War Hawk.

MIXED FEELINGS
ABOUT FIGHTING

The *Chesapeake–Leopard* clash and the Battle
of Tippecanoe drew the attention of
Congress. Certain congressmen, such as Henry Clay,
the speaker of the U.S. House of Representatives,
wanted to take action. He and other politicians

became more impatient to strike a blow that would finally put Great Britain in its place. Many were eager to make the British pay for their hostility on the open seas and their support of Native American tribes. Because Clay and several of his colleagues were so passionately in favor of war, they were known as the War Hawks.

The War Hawks cited restricted trade, impressments, and alliances with Native Americans as key reasons for declaring war on Great Britain. In addition, Clay and his supporters saw the growing hostility as an opportunity to seize more land for the United States. They were eager to control Canada, a land rich in forests that could serve as a gateway for further western and northern settlement. The politicians also eyed Florida—an area south of the United States and controlled by the Spanish, who often relied on the British

"Let war therefore be forthwith proclaimed against England. With her there can be no motive for delay. Any further discussion, any new attempt at negotiation, would be as fruitless as it would be dishonorable."[1]
—*Henry Clay,*
in a letter written in 1812

In Favor of War

Another well-known War Hawk was John C. Calhoun, a U.S. representative from South Carolina. In December 1811, he gave a famous speech before Congress explaining why war was both necessary and worthwhile. He declared, "I . . . will not . . . pretend to estimate in dollars and cents the value of national independence, or national affection. I cannot dare to measure, in shillings or pence, the misery, the stripes, and the slavery of our impressed seamen; nor even to value our shipping, commercial and agricultural losses . . . under the British system of blockade."[2]

for protection. If Great Britain were forced out of North America entirely, the continent would be open to undeterred U.S. expansion.

In the fall of 1811, President James Madison instructed Congress to take all necessary steps to ensure the United States was ready for armed conflict with Great Britain. The War Hawks wasted no time in seeing that the president's orders were carried out. They planned to increase the size of the army to 35,000 men and to call on 50,000 one-year volunteers and 100,000 militia members. Congress also increased military spending to construct coastal defenses and to prepare the navy for war.

AN IMPORTANT MESSAGE

None of these plans would be completed in time, however. In early June 1812, Madison asked Congress to issue an official declaration of war against Great Britain. The House of Representatives, led by Clay, quickly voted in favor of doing so. The Senate was a little more divided but ultimately agreed to the president's request. On June 18, 1812, the United States formally declared war on Great Britain.

Tragically, congressmen might have voted differently if communication across the Atlantic Ocean had been quicker and more reliable. During the early nineteenth century, sending a message overseas was extremely

James Madison and the Federalists

James Madison was born in 1751 in Virginia. He was small in stature, standing barely five and a half feet (1.7 m) tall. During his school years, he studied history, government, and law. He played an active role in Virginia politics and joined in many debates at the Constitutional Convention in Philadelphia, Pennsylvania. He later joined with John Jay and Alexander Hamilton to write the *Federalist Papers*, which promoted ratification of the new U.S. Constitution. During this time, Madison favored a strong central government.

However, in the 1790s, Madison began to oppose Hamilton's ideas about finance. Madison joined with Thomas Jefferson to form the Democratic-Republican Party. Madison was secretary of state during Jefferson's presidency from 1801 to 1809. He then became president in 1809.

By the time of the War of 1812, Madison had again begun to favor a strong central government. Nonetheless, he was directly opposed by members of the Federalist Party, who saw the war as benefiting other political parties and not the nation as a whole. Federalists felt that Great Britain was a vital U.S. trading partner and feared that Madison foolishly favored France and its powerful leader, Napoléon Bonaparte.

difficult and slow. Transporting handwritten notes and publications by ship was a primary means of sharing information. As a result, no one in the United States knew about an important announcement by Lord Castlereagh, Great Britain's secretary of state for foreign affairs. He stated his nation would temporarily suspend all naval blockades of France and its allies. This meant the United States would be able to resume unrestricted trade with a large portion of Europe. Castlereagh made this announcement on June 16, 1812—two days before the United States officially declared war. Yet, Americans did not receive word of Castlereagh's announcement until mid-August—61 days later. By that point, fighting between U.S. and British soldiers was well underway.

Military Resources

Neither the United States nor Great Britain was well prepared for

The Congressmen Vote

Seventy-nine members of the House of Representatives voted in favor of the War of 1812, while 49 opposed it. The votes were even closer in the Senate, where 19 politicians were in favor of going to war and 13 were not. Debate about the War of 1812 resulted in the closest congressional vote on any war in U.S. history, even to this day.

American fleet   **English fleet**

These ships symbolize the difference between the sizes of the American and British fleets at the start of the War of 1812.

the War of 1812. While the British had a powerful navy, their troops were scattered throughout Europe and in several colonies on other continents. Fighting France strained Great Britain's military resources, which suddenly had to be divided even further.

Nonetheless, the United States could not claim any great advantage. Despite the War Hawks' best planning, only about 10,000 soldiers were able to begin battle, and many lacked formal training. Madison and U.S. legislators also needed to provide funds to pay for ammunition, food, supplies, and the troops' wages. In addition, not everyone in the United States was as enthusiastic as Madison and Clay about engaging the British in combat.

COMPLAINTS ABOUT THE CONFLICT

Many Americans were against the 1812 conflict with Great Britain and often referred to it as "Mr. Madison's War."[3] They resented that the president had pushed Congress so hard to formally declare the British as the Americans' enemy. They argued Madison was more interested in expanding the borders of the United States than fighting the British for forcing U.S. sailors into naval service.

Politicians in New York and New England— especially in Connecticut, Rhode Island, and Massachusetts—were also opposed to the war. They believed businesses in their area had already suffered enough as a result of the trade restrictions in the early 1800s. In their view, the war would only further drain resources. They also realized commerce could very well be affected for several years to come. After all, nobody knew how long the war would last.

As a result, the governors of Connecticut, Massachusetts, and Rhode Island did whatever they could to protest the war. The most dramatic example occurred when they refused to send members of their state militias into combat. And merchants in New England continued to trade with the British.

The United States was anxious to reestablish safety and free trade on the high seas. It was also eager to gain control of Canada and new territories in the south and west. Just as important, Madison and several congressmen hoped to at last rid the United States of British influence.

In the summer of 1812, Madison and his generals finalized their plan of attack. However, the United States'

Fear of the Future

Some well-known Americans, such as journalist William Coleman, did not hesitate to express their unhappiness with the idea of fighting another war against the British. In 1811, in an article for the *New York Evening Post*, he wrote, "The conflict will be long and severe: resistance formidable, and the final result doubtful. A nation that can debar the conqueror of Europe [Napoléon Bonaparte] from the sea, and resist his armies in Spain, will not surrender its provinces without a struggle."[4]

earliest attempts at land warfare would result in failure, discouragement, and further questioning of the conflict, which would continue throughout the war. ⟶

Lord Castlereagh's announcement could have prevented a U.S. declaration of war, but the news was received too late.

Isaac Brock was the British commander of Upper Canada during the War of 1812.

FALLEN FORTS AND SURPRISING SHIPS

President Madison's initial ideas for defeating the British focused largely on invading Canada. In 1812, only 7,000 British soldiers were ready to defend this huge, largely unsettled section of North America. Lieutenant

General George Prevost and Major General Isaac Brock were the British officials in Canada in charge of the troops.

President Madison worked with his military advisers to create a three-part strategy for overtaking the British in Canada. The Americans would invade from three places: near present-day Detroit, Michigan; along the Niagara Peninsula in what is now Ontario, Canada; and in Montreal, Canada, by way of Lake Champlain in New York.

The Detroit attack was led by William Hull, the governor of the Michigan Territory and a brigadier general. He successfully entered British territory. However, the news that the small U.S. outpost at Mackinac Island (now part of Michigan) had surrendered shook his confidence. He was also uneasy about possibly being attacked by Tecumseh and his Native American warriors. Hull was aware that a significant number of local tribes had already declared themselves Great Britain's allies. Surrounded by the British, Hull surrendered Fort Detroit and the 2,000 soldiers who were responsible for defending it to Brock on August 16.

This loss weakened U.S. confidence and strengthened British enthusiasm for the war.

Hull's actions had other consequences as well. Before surrendering Detroit, he had ordered the evacuation of Fort Dearborn in what is now Chicago, Illinois. It was a decision made in a moment of panic that proved disastrous to the troops and civilians stationed there. Soon after leaving the fort, nearly half of them died and the rest fell prisoner in an attack by Potawatomi Indians.

DISASTER, DEFEAT, AND DISGRACE

Not long after Fort Detroit fell to the British, Major General Stephen Van Rensselaer began preparing about 6,000 U.S. troops to attack along the Niagara frontier. The general lacked experience and supplies. Even so, on October 13, 1812, his army initially appeared to have the upper hand in the fighting in Queenston Heights, located in present-day Ontario, Canada. As the combat raged on, Brock was

Native American Victory

The U.S. losses at Fort Detroit and Fort Dearborn were more than victories for the British. Tecumseh also benefited as the defeats motivated more Native Americans to band together under his leadership. In particular, several groups living along the upper Mississippi River and the Missouri River joined Tecumseh's confederation of tribes following early U.S. defeats.

shot and killed. The British had lost one of their most prized commanders. Then, the British began a counterattack later in the day. They beat back the Americans, who ultimately had to surrender. One of the main reasons for this turn of events was that troops from the New York militia refused to enter Canada to fight.

On the other hand, some U.S. officers were willing to fight but incapable of winning. General Henry Dearborn, who commanded an attack on Montreal, was slow

Regular Soldiers versus Trained Civilians

The United States used both state militias and the nation's regular army during the War of 1812. Militiamen were usually ordinary civilians with varying levels of military training, while members of the U.S. Army were professional, well-trained soldiers.

This difference often caused conflicts among the troops. For example, Van Rensselaer had a difficult time earning the respect of some of his fellow officers as he prepared for the Battle of Queenston Heights. He held rank in a state militia, which made some commanders within the regular army look down on him. They did not believe Van Rensselaer could match their experience with or knowledge of combat.

In some cases, militiamen did not willingly follow and obey officers whose backgrounds were with the regular army. Because militias were state based, militiamen often viewed fighting outside their home states as being beyond their duty. Members of New York's militia steadfastly refused to engage in combat on Canadian soil.

The New York militiamen were also aware that their state government did not support the war and had been reluctant to send the local militia into battle. This knowledge, combined with the overall difference between militiamen and career soldiers, had a significant impact on the outcome of the Battle of Queenston Heights.

General Henry Dearborn in 1812

to take action and often hesitated to make important decisions. The militiamen in his campaign were unruly. And by November 1812, he had completely abandoned the idea of attacking Montreal. The failure appeared to mark the final blow in the United States' early attempts to invade Canada.

The U.S. forces' repeated defeats on North American soil were extremely disheartening to

Americans. Those who had opposed the War of 1812 from the beginning believed the losses proved that President Madison and Clay had set the nation on a path that would end only in devastation. As one U.S. newspaper reported, the plan to assault Canada was filled with "disaster, defeat, disgrace, and ruin and death."[1]

Yet, despite its many setbacks, the United States was not ready to give up. While U.S. troops may have failed on land, they were surprisingly successful on water.

U.S. Successes on the High Seas

There was no denying Great Britain's Royal Navy was impressive. The British military fleet boasted more than 1,000 vessels. It had also earned a reputation for being powerful and, in times of war, remarkably destructive. In 1812, however, Great Britain had to divide its naval resources among areas all over the globe. At the time, the British were battling both the United States and France and its allies.

As a result, only a handful of British ships were available to face the U.S. fleet. Some U.S. military advisers were doubtful that the collection of U.S.

vessels would ever prove a match for the Royal Navy. Yet, bold U.S. captains such as Isaac Hull, Stephen Decatur, and William Bainbridge strongly disagreed.

Hull commanded the USS *Constitution*. As it cut through Atlantic waters on August 19, 1812, its crew happened to see the HMS *Guerrière*. British captain James R. Dacres was in command of the *Guerrière*. He was well known for his scornful attitude toward the U.S. Navy. Armed with 54 guns, the *Constitution* blasted the *Guerrière* with cannon fire for more than two hours. The British ship fired back, but even cannonballs seemed to do little damage to the U.S. vessel. A sailor aboard the *Constitution* could barely contain his excitement upon seeing the strength of the U.S. frigate. "Huzza!" the serviceman was reported to shout. "Her sides are made of iron."[2] Because of this remark, the *Constitution*

Impressive Naval Victory

Americans were excited about their impressive and somewhat unexpected victories over the mighty Royal Navy in 1812. "British arms cannot withstand American upon the sea," boasted one congressman. "The bully has been disgraced by an infant."[3]

was given the nickname "Old Ironsides."

The *Constitution* was not the only U.S. frigate to triumph over the Royal Navy in 1812. In October of that year, Decatur led the USS *United States* to victory off Africa's northwestern shore. Both the United States and Great Britain had naval vessels sailing around the globe. That meant warfare between the two nations was not restricted to U.S. or European waters. Decatur and his crew forced British captain John S. Carden and the HMS *Macedonian* to surrender on October 25, 1812.

Bainbridge also experienced the satisfaction of defeating the enemy. In December 1812, he led the USS *Constitution* to victory over the HMS *Java* along the coast of Brazil. Both the British and the Americans put up a determined and courageous fight, and both ships sustained serious damage. Bainbridge was wounded

USS *Constitution*

Two centuries after surviving an attack by British cannonballs, the USS *Constitution* is still afloat in Boston Harbor. There, visitors can tour the warship and the USS Constitution Museum, located nearby in Charlestown, Massachusetts. People are encouraged to study the vessel and related exhibits to learn what life was like for nineteenth-century sailors—including the crew who battled the *Guerrière* in 1812.

Privateers

Warships known as privateers also played a role in the War of 1812. These privately owned vessels were not part of either side's official navy. Rather, they were hired by a national government, such as Great Britain, to attack and take goods from boats involved in trading and shipping conducted by the enemy. Privateers could severely affect a country's ability to transport goods. Privateers also forced nations at war to devote additional forces to protecting their nonmilitary ships.

twice, and British captain Henry Lambert was one of several men who lost their lives aboard the *Java.* In the end, the Americans won the battle. After taking the *Java*'s crew as prisoners, they sank the British ship. As 1812 drew to a close, however, it was still unclear whether the United States or Great Britain was winning a war that showed few signs of being over.

Today, the USS Constitution is anchored in the Charlestown Navy Yard.

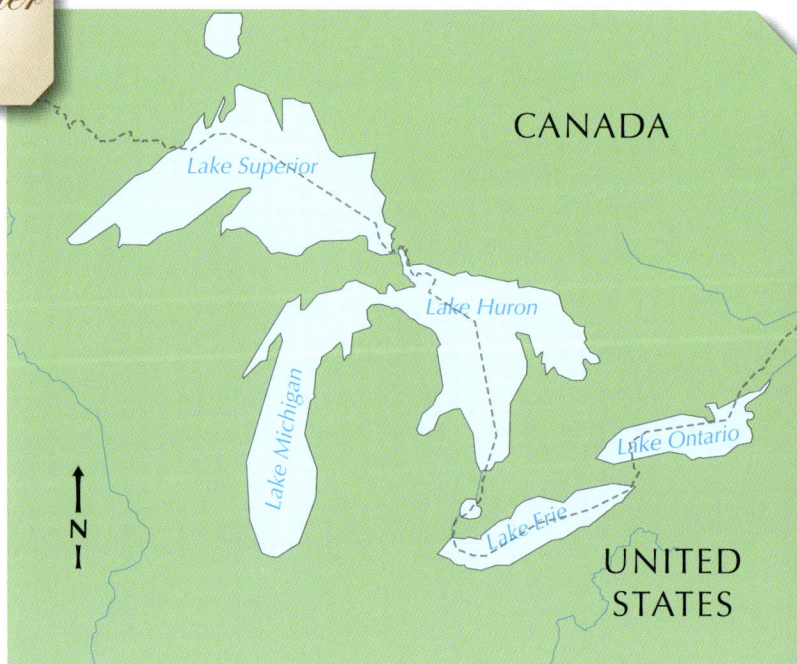

Chapter 5

---- *Modern-day U.S.–Canadian Border*

During the War of 1812, the United States and Great Britain battled for control of the Great Lakes.

From the Northwest to the Southeast

The first year of the war had not been an easy one for the United States. By 1813, however, U.S. military forces were stronger and more organized. The number of servicemen had increased. Also, a handful of bright, energetic, young commanders, such as Harrison and Jackson, had begun playing larger roles. For many Americans, these changes made victory seem more likely. To win the war, however, the United States first had to take control of the Great Lakes.

Control of these waterways was important for two reasons. First, they bordered large portions of the Old Northwest territory and Canada—lands prized by both the United States and Great Britain. Second, the Great Lakes served as an important means of transporting goods and supplies throughout these areas. The British claimed authority over the Great Lakes in 1812. By seizing them, U.S. soldiers could cut off major supply lines the British depended on. Of the five Great Lakes, Lake Erie and Lake Ontario were considered of particular strategic value.

Overtaking Great Britain's fleet would not be simple, however. The Royal Navy had approximately a dozen vessels stationed on the Great Lakes, while the United States had only one warship sailing on Lake Ontario. The United States would have to buy and build more boats.

In late April 1813, U.S. Navy Captain Isaac Chauncey and General Zebulon Pike organized an assault off the waters of Lake Ontario. They

American Army general Zebulon Pike

succeeded in capturing York, a major British
stronghold located in present-day Toronto, Canada.
Pike was killed during the invasion. After the
victory, U.S. troops proceeded to loot and burn
the surrounding community. The British were

enraged by this behavior and bitter at losing control of Lake Ontario. The day would come when the British would prove to the Americans just how insulting their actions were at York. In the meantime, however, the United States temporarily had the upper hand in the war.

THE BRITISH LOSS OF LAKE ERIE

More than a year after Congress declared war on Great Britain, the fighting raged on. Combat was intense on Lake Erie in September 1813. U.S. naval officer Oliver Hazard Perry had managed to put together a nine-ship fleet. He planned on using it to overpower Captain Robert H. Barclay of the Royal Navy on September 10.

Zebulon Pike

Before becoming involved in the War of 1812, Zebulon Pike had explored the West in 1805. Pike's Peak in Colorado is named for him.

Pike took his role as a U.S. general seriously. He was ready and willing to sacrifice his life in the service of his country. He expressed his dedication in a letter he wrote to his father shortly before he died during the invasion of York in the spring of 1813: "If success attends my steps, honor and glory await my name; if defeat, still shall it be said we died like brave men, and conferred honor even in death on the American name."[1]

The British officer commanded six vessels on the lake. However, recent events had made him question whether he could withstand a U.S. assault. The previous July, Great Britain had tried to push south from Canada into Ohio, but U.S. troops had turned back both the British troops and their Native American allies.

Months later, Barclay and his fleet sailed the waters of Lake Erie. They were aware of the defeat in Ohio but dangerously in need of supplies. Both the British and U.S. navies were put to the test during a bloody and destructive battle. Intense gunfire destroyed the USS *Lawrence*, Perry's flagship, within a matter of hours, but Perry refused to give up.

Perry boarded the USS *Niagara* and rallied his

U.S. Actions at York

More than a year after the Battle of York, the British captured and burned Washington DC. Their destruction of the U.S. capital was a terrifying moment for Americans across the nation. Many citizens did not stop and consider, however, that their own troops had behaved similarly in the spring of 1813.

At York, chaos erupted after U.S. soldiers overpowered British forces. The Americans were devastated by the loss of their commander, General Zebulon Pike, who died in the attack. For U.S. troops, destroying the Canadian settlement at York was the perfect way to punish the British for Pike's death. Destroying York also gave U.S. troops the chance to get even for their own defeats by the British and acts of cruelty believed to have been committed by Native Americans.

So, the U.S. troops did not hesitate to burn and vandalize both private and public property. They also looted local homes and businesses, stealing a variety of valuables. Dearborn and other U.S. commanders would eventually criticize such actions. However, there is little evidence that the commanders did much to discourage them at the time.

British emotions were far clearer. Great Britain's deep anger with its enemy would become obvious when its troops made their way to Washington DC later in the war.

men onward. He urged even injured sailors to help finish off the badly damaged British ships the HMS *Queen Charlotte* and the HMS *Detroit*. The troops rose to the challenge, and Barclay, himself severely wounded, surrendered Lake Erie. Perry wasted no time in scribbling a note that described the victory to Harrison, who was in charge of U.S. military efforts in the northwest. "We have met the enemy and they are ours," he proclaimed.[2]

The United States' gaining control of Lake Erie was extremely significant. It meant the British were no longer able to supply or reinforce their troops in the western Great Lakes. Additional U.S. successes in both this area and the southeast would follow throughout the autumn of 1813.

IMPACTS ON NATIVE AMERICANS

Thanks in part to Perry's achievements on Lake Erie, Harrison was able to reclaim Detroit

Perry's Fleet on Lake Erie

Oliver Hazard Perry oversaw the construction of four vessels out of his fleet of nine, including the *Niagara*. His shipbuilding activities on Lake Erie represented quite an accomplishment, as the surrounding area lacked the population and industry of a major city. The U.S. commander had to arrange for craftsmen and materials to be brought in from other parts of the country, such as Pennsylvania, New York, and Washington DC.

in September 1813. He then headed east, catching up with enemy forces 50 miles (80 km) away, at the settlement of Moraviantown. The British were fleeing to Canada after their unsuccessful attempt at invading the northwest. The resulting battle along the Thames River on October 5, 1813, became known as the Battle of the Thames. The U.S. victory there allowed the country to win back territory in the northwest that it had lost during the early stages of the war.

Not only was the Battle of the Thames a serious defeat for the British, but it also had major long-term effects on their Native American allies. Tecumseh, the famous Shawnee leader, was killed at Moraviantown. After his death, tribes who had belonged to his confederation began to lose their sense of purpose and unity. In the following years, these tribes entered into a number of treaties with the United States. The result was a gradual loss of their territories and overall way of life. Native Americans' confidence was further shaken by events that had been unfolding in the southeast since the previous summer.

Months before the Battle of the Thames, a Creek chief named Red Eagle had led an attack that killed

247 white settlers at Fort Mims, in what is now the state of Alabama. A response to earlier white aggression, the attack proved significant. It made white settlers in the area deeply uneasy. It also served as a reminder of the obstacles to further national expansion.

In response, General Jackson was ordered to go after Red Eagle and his band of fierce Creek warriors called Red Sticks. The hostilities that followed lasted several months. Jackson and his troops attacked and defeated various parts of the tribe in the fall of 1813. Then, in March 1814, he finally triumphed over Red Eagle at the Battle of Horseshoe Bend on the Tallapoosa River in present-day Alabama. Red Eagle surrendered himself to Jackson.

The fact that the United States had won additional territory in the southeast was unquestionably a blow to the British. However, the

Native American Allies

Not all Native Americans helped the British fight the United States during the War of 1812. When Jackson marched against the Red Sticks in 1813 and 1814, he was joined by members of the Choctaw, Cherokee, and Chickasaw tribes, as well as many Creeks who did not support Red Eagle.

Some Native Americans believed that working with, rather than against, U.S. officials was the best way to preserve their lands and to promote lasting peace. Unfortunately, after the Treaty of Fort Jackson in 1814, lands were taken from these U.S. allies and from the Creeks who had fought with Red Eagle.

U.S. military's triumphs over Native Americans greatly changed relations between these two groups. Defeated tribal leaders later signed the Treaty of Fort Jackson. It proclaimed their people would give up 23 million acres (9.3 million ha) of their land to the U.S. government.

The United States had completed its conquest of Native American lands east of the Mississippi. But as was true during the first stages of the War of 1812, neither side could boast clear victory. The United States was victorious on the Great Lakes and in the south. Great Britain started strengthening its naval presence along its enemy's shores.

Chief Red Eagle surrendered to General Jackson after the Battle of Horseshoe Bend.

British ships blockading Chesapeake Bay during the War of 1812

BRITAIN'S RESPONSE TO U.S. ENEMIES

During 1813, the United States had won back control of the northwest and had begun gaining territory in the southeast. Even so, Great Britain had managed to stop U.S. advances in Canada. In autumn, the British turned back two

U.S. armies that intended to capture the important Canadian city of Montreal. In December, the British also reclaimed control of the Niagara frontier by pushing U.S. invaders out of Canada and burning U.S. towns such as Black Rock and Buffalo in New York. In addition to these losses, the Americans had to deal with a rapidly deteriorating situation on the high seas.

The British had stationed more of the Royal Navy in North American waters. As a result, they were gradually able to tighten their blockade of the U.S. coastline. The move crippled the United States' ability to trade overseas and to launch warships from Atlantic ports. Faced with a growing economic crisis, many Americans became increasingly critical of the War of 1812. They wondered why President Madison and his generals were trying so hard to beat the British if it meant U.S. citizens had to sacrifice everything, from personal security to financial prosperity.

Added to this were several naval defeats on the Atlantic Ocean. One such ill-fated fight occurred between the USS *Chesapeake* and the HMS *Shannon* on June 1, 1813. James Lawrence and his men had left Boston, Massachusetts, to attack British Captain

Philip Broke and his crew. The Americans were aboard the same vessel involved in the *Chesapeake-Leopard* battle of 1807. They were no match for the well-trained, well-armed crew of the *Shannon*.

After French emperor Napoléon Bonaparte fell from power in the spring of 1814, the outlook seemed even bleaker for the United States. Because the British were no longer fighting the French, they were able to send even more forces across the ocean to fight the United States.

Battle of Chippewa

The courage and skill of U.S. troops during the Battle of Chippewa both stunned and impressed the British. Before the fighting, British commander Phineas Riall had incorrectly assumed he would be facing poorly trained militiamen, not U.S. Army regulars. Historians believe this may have led Riall to be overly confident when he attacked. As U.S. forces stood firm against the enemy's intense artillery fire, Riall realized he was facing professional soldiers who clearly knew how to wage a fierce fight.

A Stronger Enemy

The British boldly planned a threefold attack. In 1814, they plotted assaults against U.S. troops near the Canadian border, in Chesapeake Bay, and in the Gulf of Mexico. But before the British could begin their invasions, they had to deal with a renewed U.S. offensive on the Niagara frontier.

On July 5, 1814, 3,500 U.S. troops clashed with a British force of 2,800 at the Battle of Chippewa.

The U.S. soldiers displayed tremendous discipline and bravery, forcing the enemy to retreat. On July 25, the Battle of Lundy's Lane erupted near Niagara Falls. At the end of this fierce battle, however, it was less clear which nation had won. Both Great Britain and the United States suffered serious losses.

In the following weeks, the British stationed more troops in other parts of North America. In August, an estimated 4,500 British soldiers arrived in Maryland. As British warships dropped anchor in Chesapeake Bay, U.S. citizens were forced to realize that their enemy was creeping closer toward Washington DC.

CRISIS IN THE CAPITAL

More than a year after U.S. forces captured, burned, and looted York, British forces had not forgotten the insult and were in a position to take

A Gruesome Fight

The Battle of Lundy's Lane was one of the most brutal episodes of combat to occur during the War of 1812. After the fighting ended, one British lieutenant recalled the grim sights and sounds that surrounded him. "I assure you," he noted, "I never passed so awful a night as that of the action. The stillness of the evening after the firing ceased, the Groans of the dying and wounded. . . . I was cold and wretched, what must not have been the misery of those Unfortunates who remained on the Field. A Soldier's life is very horrid sometimes."[1]

revenge. As the British inched nearer to the U.S. capital in the summer of 1814, U.S. troops situated on the Maryland–Washington DC border began to lose their nerve.

While a small number of the troops tried to turn back the advancing enemy, many mistakes were made in preparing for the invasion. The poorly defended capital became an easy target for the British soldiers who made their way there on August 24, 1814. Madison and several of his advisers hastily fled the White House and took refuge in the nearby countryside. First Lady Dolley Madison departed soon afterward. But first, she quickly packed a handful of key government documents, including the original drafts of the Declaration of Independence and the U.S. Constitution.

Mrs. Madison had predicted that the British commanders would show

Retaliation

Great Britain's soldiers admittedly had revenge on their minds when they made their way to Washington DC in 1814. Their fury at U.S. actions following the Battle of York had not diminished over time. As British Lieutenant General George Prevost explained, his forces hoped to use invasions launched from the bay as a means of "inflicting that measure of retaliation which shall deter the enemy from the repetition of similar outrages."[2]

First Lady Dolley Madison saved the Declaration of Independence
and other important documents.

little respect for U.S. treasures, and she was correct.
As one British officer later recalled,

> We entered Washington for the barbarous purpose of
> destroying the city. . . . In the [White House], however,

we found a supper all ready . . . which many of us speedily consumed . . . and [we] drank some very good wine also. I shall never forget the destructive majesty of the flames as the torches were applied to the beds, curtains, etc. Our sailors were artists at the work.[3]

The invaders proved equally skilled when it came to burning various government buildings.

When the British abandoned the capital days later, they had managed to destroy more than just property. Americans across the nation received news of the devastation and the president's flight with a mixture of terror and hopelessness.

The War Drags On

After two years of fighting, the country's morale was low. Not only that, funding the war had become an issue. Not even the War Hawks had imagined the conflict would last so long, and the war's initial budget was no longer realistic. In addition, the economy was suffering as a result of continued trade restrictions.

In September 1814, however, Americans' spirits were boosted by a series of significant victories. On September 11, U.S. forces prevented the British from seizing control of Lake Champlain and advancing into Albany, New York, and the Hudson River Valley.

U.S. troops also successfully fought back Great Britain's attempted invasion of Maryland's Baltimore Harbor. This was the battle that prompted Francis Scott Key to write his famous poem that became "The Star-Spangled Banner."

It was slowly becoming obvious that neither the British nor the Americans were moving closer to overtaking the other's territories. In addition, both

Leaving Washington DC Defenseless

Americans did not think of protecting their capital from British invasion.

Secretary of War John Armstrong did not believe Great Britain had much interest in seizing Washington DC. The U.S. government had only designated Washington DC the nation's permanent capital in 1790. Then, another decade passed before lawmakers and other officials actually began conducting most of their political business there. Only a handful of federal buildings stood in Washington DC. Baltimore, however, was a major seaport. In addition, several U.S. warships were being built along Maryland's coast. Armstrong thought enemy troops would be far more likely to attack Baltimore.

Unfortunately, by the time Armstrong and his commanders realized their error in judgment, Washington DC was basically defenseless. U.S. officers had already exchanged incorrect reports about the size and progress of the approaching British troops. One group of U.S. forces had hoped to prevent enemy soldiers from entering the capital by first defeating them at the nearby town of Bladensburg, Maryland. The British quickly overwhelmed these forces.

The British were delighted by their humiliation of the Americans and eager to repay them for their behavior at York. British forces soon marched on toward Washington DC.

nations were growing exhausted of combat and suffering the economic side effects of the war. Given all this, by late 1814, the idea of negotiating peace appealed to many people on both sides of the war. Yet, talk of a possible treaty between Great Britain and the United States did not develop into action. One particularly important battle remained to be fought before the War of 1812 would finally draw to an end. ⌐

British soldiers largely destroyed the White House when they
set fire to it during the War of 1812.

Signatures on the Treaty of Ghent

PEACE TALKS AND CONTINUED COMBAT

reat Britain and the United States had
made various halfhearted attempts to
negotiate peace since 1813. However, during the late
summer of the following year, each nation began
to put forth a more serious effort. In August 1814,

British and U.S. officials met in the port city of Ghent (in present-day Belgium, but at the time controlled by the Netherlands) to discuss possible terms of a treaty.

The Debate at Ghent

Once at Ghent, however, officials from the two sides often had a hard time seeing eye to eye. For instance, the British felt strongly about setting aside land near the Great Lakes where Native Americans could live in peace. In reality, though, the British wanted to establish an area of neutral ground between its Canadian settlements and U.S. territories in the northwest. In addition, British diplomats were eager for the United States to diminish its military presence on the Great Lakes. The British also wanted access to the Mississippi River and ownership of parts of New York and other areas close to Canada. Not surprisingly, U.S. ambassadors were

U.S. Representatives in Ghent

President Madison sent several U.S. diplomats across the Atlantic Ocean to attend the meeting in Ghent. They included John Quincy Adams (who was then acting as ambassador to Russia), Secretary of the Treasury Albert Gallatin, Senator John Bayard of Delaware, the U.S. Charge in London and ambassador to Sweden Jonathan Russell, and Speaker of the House of Representatives Henry Clay.

Louisiana Climate

The British soldiers who were stationed in the Gulf Coast in 1814 came from various military posts in the Caribbean Sea. After arriving in Louisiana, they had a difficult time adjusting to the landscape and climate. The area was filled with swamps and bogs, and the air was both humid and cold as winter began.

British captain George Gleig summed up the area in this report: "It is scarcely possible to imagine any place more completely wretched. It was a swamp, containing a small space of firm ground at one end, and almost wholly unadorned with trees of any sort or description. . . . To add to our miseries, as night closed, the rain generally ceased, and severe frosts set in."[1]

not eager to submit to all of Great Britain's requests.

For their part, U.S. officials took up the issue of impressment. They demanded that Great Britain pay the United States compensation for any unjustly captured ships and crews. U.S. diplomats also argued that the British needed to rethink their use of wartime blockades.

While diplomats debated at Ghent, fighting continued in North America. As fall approached, soldiers on both sides of the conflict started readying for what promised to be intense combat in New Orleans, Louisiana.

PROTECTING LOUISIANA'S PRIZED PORT

Louisiana became a state in 1812, just months before Congress officially declared war on Great Britain. This state had important strategic value, as it contained the port city of New

Orleans. Located at the mouth of the Mississippi River and along the Gulf of Mexico, New Orleans offered control of the United States' most important river. Controlling the city and thus the river would provide countless benefits in terms of trade and military advantage.

It was commonly believed that if New Orleans fell into British hands, the United States' chances of winning the War of 1812 would be seriously reduced. Amazingly, however, the United States had done little to secure

The Pirate Who Helped Protect New Orleans

Countless heroes and legends were created by the War of 1812—among them, Jean Lafitte and his adventures on the high seas. Details about this pirate's life are somewhat unclear. He was probably born during the 1780s in France or one of its Caribbean colonies.

By 1814, Lafitte had developed a reputation for smuggling slaves and a variety of goods into the United States. Much of his activity was based in Louisiana. He provided Americans with items they often could not get because of trade restrictions with Great Britain. Lafitte was also a privateer hired by different countries to attack their enemies' merchant ships.

Therefore, Lafitte had several run-ins with the law. By the final stages of the War of 1812, however, Lafitte offered to assist Jackson in protecting New Orleans. He hoped providing military support would help win pardons for him and several of his fellow pirates.

Desperate to strengthen New Orleans's defenses, Jackson agreed to these terms. In turn, Lafitte supplied extra ammunition and a band of fearless fighters who were familiar with Louisiana's Gulf Coast. At first, Jackson had little respect for a man he considered a reckless bandit. But he later acknowledged that the clever pirate played an important role in helping overcome the British assault on New Orleans.

the port by late 1814. As the British had proved in Washington DC, they would not hesitate to destroy a poorly defended U.S. city.

Then, in December 1814, General Jackson arrived in New Orleans. Famous for his bravery and fiery spirit, the southern commander was determined to protect Louisiana's key port. Upon arriving in the city, Jackson vowed that he would "drive [the country's] enemies into the sea or perish in the effort."[2]

While few people doubted Jackson's sincerity, most believed that turning back the British would be difficult. Jackson had far fewer troops than the British. He commanded only 4,000 to 5,000 men. In addition, Jackson's troops had a wide range of backgrounds and levels of training. The U.S. forces included members of different state militias, along with African Americans, Native Americans, Frenchmen, and even a handful of pirates, including Jean Lafitte.

British commander Major General Edward Pakenham's troops far outnumbered Jackson's. Estimates vary, but historians believe there were approximately 8,000 British troops in the area. Most of these men were well-trained soldiers who

The British offered pirate Jean Lafitte money and a pardon to help them attack New Orleans, but he aided the United States instead.

had served in the Napoleonic Wars in Europe. Even so, as the city of New Orleans prepared for attack, Jackson and his troops became even more committed to driving the British back into the sea.

A Final Fight

Weeks before a single shot was fired in New Orleans, U.S. forces worked hard to defend the port from a British assault. Jackson declared the city was under martial law, or control of the military. This meant that all residents had to obey curfews and other rules that Jackson and his commanders handed down. Jackson's forces also blocked access to waterways leading into the area. Then, he and his men waited to see exactly how, when, and where the British would attack.

On December 13, 1814, the waiting ended. That day, a British fleet forced its way from the Gulf of Mexico onto Lake Borgne, a body of water north of New Orleans. Despite all the preparations, U.S. gunboats had failed to hold back the enemy. Refusing to accept failure, Jackson rallied his soldiers. He ordered them to attack the invaders on December 14.

The fighting went on for several weeks. Even though Jackson's

British Casualties in New Orleans

The British troops suffered many casualties at the Battle of New Orleans. As one British officer recollected, "Prompted by curiosity, I mounted my horse and rode to the front; but of all the sights I ever witnessed, that which met me there was beyond comparison the most shocking and the most humiliating. Within the narrow compass of a few hundred yards, were gathered together nearly a thousand bodies, all of them arrayed in British uniforms."[3]

troops were outnumbered and undertrained, they had one clear advantage over the British: They were battling on their own soil. The U.S. troops were comfortable making their way through the area's foggy bayous and soggy marshes. They knew the land well and were able to use this knowledge to launch surprise attacks.

As Great Britain and the United States struggled for control of New Orleans, the New Year came and went. Then, on January 8, 1815, one battle decided the future of the city and the end of formal combat in the War of 1812. In the Battle of New Orleans, Jackson's troops were able to drive the British back into Lake Borgne and ultimately out of Louisiana. It was a devastating defeat for the British, who suffered many casualties.

By 1815, both Great Britain and the United States were weary of the war. Yet, during the Battle of

Victory Song

In the nineteenth century, people often spread information about major events through newspaper articles, cartoons, poems, and songs. The following song, entitled "The Eighth of January," was composed shortly after the Battle of New Orleans. It describes the American offense, called "Yankee play," and victory over the British:

"Remember New Orleans I say, / Where Jackson [showed] them Yankee play, / And beat them off and [gained] the day, / And then we heard the people say / Huzza! For [General] Jackson."[4]

New Orleans, each side put up an aggressive and determined fight. Tragically, though, this fighting did not need to happen. Just two weeks earlier, and after four months of talks, U.S. and British diplomats signed the peace Treaty of Ghent on December 24, 1814.

General Jackson, on horseback, led his troops to victory
in the Battle of New Orleans.

The Battle of New Orleans was more important to Jackson's future than to the outcome of the war.

ENDING THE CONFLICT

Jackson and his men rejoiced at winning the Battle of New Orleans. Many Americans, however, were not even aware of the triumph. In 1815, news still traveled slowly, so few Americans outside the South knew about the victory in

Louisiana. Tension grew as people across the United States waited to hear whether Jackson had successfully defended the valuable port. As people awaited word, rumors and incorrect information added to their anxiety.

News from the Netherlands

By late 1814, U.S. politicians who opposed the war were finding it increasingly difficult to justify the sacrifices Americans had made. Likewise, they were finding it hard to justify the $93 million the government had spent on the military since 1812. These politicians, who were mainly from New England, gathered in Hartford, Connecticut, in December and January for a meeting that became known as the Hartford Convention. Rumors swirled as the attendees conducted secretive discussions about how to respond to the war. Some people even hinted that certain states were

Delayed News

It was not until early February 1815 that Americans in New England and nearby states discovered that Jackson's troops had triumphed in the Battle of New Orleans. British subjects did not learn of Jackson's victory until even later.

considering seceding from the United States in protest.

As the winter of 1815 progressed, word of Jackson's success in New Orleans lifted Americans' spirits. Then, on February 11, 1815, the British ship HMS *Favorite* docked in the harbor outside New York City. Americans quickly realized they had no reason to fear the arrival of the British vessel. Aboard the ship were messengers who brought the news about the signed peace Treaty of Ghent. The news spread like wildfire.

The treaty had been signed weeks before the Battle of

Demands from the Hartford Convention

Delegates who attended the Hartford Convention eventually created a list of demands they intended to present to government leaders in Washington DC. Many of these delegates were members of the Federalist Party. Their main goal was to get financial assistance to rebuild New England's economy, which had been hurt by years of trade restrictions.

In addition, these politicians were eager for Congress to set rules for voting on government actions. Specifically, they wanted a rule requiring at least two-thirds of congressmen to vote in favor of declaring war or passing a trade embargo before such an action could take place.

Unfortunately for the Federalists who met in Hartford, their list made its way to Washington DC at about the same time as news of the U.S. victory at New Orleans. With this news, the British threat was diminished and Americans' sense of patriotism was renewed. The complaints of the Federalists therefore failed to win much support. Furthermore, the timing of their demands made them appear unpatriotic. The Federalist Party had no real influence on the U.S. government after this time.

New Orleans, but news of both events reached the eastern United States almost simultaneously. Americans could not help but connect the two events, perhaps believing the victory in New Orleans had ended the war. Even though the treaty declared the conflict a tie, it appeared as though Jackson had won the war. Most Americans chose not to dwell on the tragic reality that the fighting had continued weeks longer than necessary. Instead, they were relieved and overjoyed that the War of 1812 had ended.

The President's Sentiments

President Madison was similarly pleased when he formally presented the peace agreement to Congress on February 18, 1815. In a speech he gave that day, the president made this statement:

> *The late war, although reluctantly declared by Congress, had become*

Peace at Any Price?

While Americans were mostly excited about reaching peace, critics of the Treaty of Ghent did not hesitate to state their dissatisfaction. In the winter of 1815, Daniel Webster, a member of the U.S. House of Representatives, wrote, "I am fearful the day of peace is still distant."[1]

a necessary resort to assert the rights and independence of the nation. It has been waged with a success which is the natural result of the wisdom of the legislative councils, of the patriotism of the people, of the public spirit of the militia, and of the valor of the military and naval forces of the country.[2]

The president went on to praise Congress and to insist that the United States had acted honorably during the entire war:

Peace, at all times a blessing, is peculiarly welcome, therefore, at a period when the causes for the war have ceased to operate, when the Government has demonstrated the efficiency of its powers of defense, and when the nation can review its conduct without regret and without reproach.[3]

Madison seemed to express a sense of victory, and most U.S. citizens enjoyed the idea of having defeated Great Britain.

U.S. Casualties

Not all the U.S. soldiers who died during the War of 1812 were killed in battle. As with all military conflicts before World War II, infection and illness also caused many deaths. According to estimates, approximately 2,260 U.S. troops died in battle in the War of 1812. Some experts believe that if all deaths related to infection and illness were also counted, U.S. casualties would probably number approximately 17,000.

The signing of the Treaty of Ghent ended the War of 1812.

WHICH SIDE WON?

Despite Americans' satisfaction with the outcome of the war, the victor was not clear. When peace negotiations were held in late 1814, diplomats found it difficult to determine if one side had actually defeated the other. Neither Great Britain nor the United States could boast much success. Neither had achieved any of the major goals it had once considered important.

For instance, two of the reasons the United States went to war with Great Britain were to end British impressments of U.S. sailors and to eliminate restrictions on U.S. trade with Europe. But in the end, the British did not agree to show Americans greater respect at sea. In turn, U.S. diplomats refused to grant any of the significant requests Great Britain made regarding land usage. This included the land the British had wanted to set aside for Native Americans.

U.S. leaders also realized that their plan to expand the nation by seizing land in Canada had failed. And while U.S. forces had won the last major battle of the war, they had lost or come away battered from many other battles. The leaders knew they had not accomplished most of the objectives they had set forth in 1812.

In the end, diplomats at the peace talks chose to postpone discussion of several topics until a later session. By late 1814, officials from both sides were more eager to end the

Artwork celebrates the peace brought about by the Treaty of Ghent.

conflict than to squabble over the details of a peace agreement. However, the main agreement reached between Great Britain and the United States was essentially that things should return to how they had been before the war.

And so, to this day, historians continue to debate which side truly won the War of 1812. Historians generally agree, however, about the important long-term consequences of the war for everyone involved in it. ⁓

Evening Gazette Office,

Boston, *Monday*, 10, *a.m.*

The following most highly important handbill has just been issued from the C**entinel** p**ress**. We deem it a duty that we owe our Friends and the Public to assist in the prompt spread of the Glorious News.

Treaty of PEACE signed and arrived.

C**entinel** *Office. Feb. 13, 1815, 8 o'clock in the morning.*

WE have this instant received in Thirty-two hours from New-York the following

Great and Happy News!

FOR THE PUBLIC.

To B**enjamin** R**ussell**, *Esq. Centinel-Office, Boston.*

New-York, Feb. 11, 1815—Saturday Evening, 10 o'clock.

SIR—

I HASTEN to acquaint you, for the information of the Public, of the arrival here this afternoon of H. Br. M. sloop of war *Favorite*, in which has come passenger Mr C**arroll**, American Messenger, having in his possession

A Treaty of Peace

Between this Country and Great-Britain, signed on the 26th December last.

Mr Baker also is on board, as Agent for the British Government, the same who was formerly Charge des Affairs here.

Mr Carroll reached town at eight o'clock this evening. He shewed to a friend of mine, who is acquainted with him, the pacquet containing the *Treaty*, and a London newspaper of the last date of December, announcing the signing of the Treaty

It depends, however, as my friend observed, upon the act of the President to suspend hostilities on this side.

The gentleman left London the 2d Jan. The *Transit* had sailed previously from a port on the Continent.

This city is in a perfect uproar of joy, shouts, illuminations, &c. &c.

I have undertaken to send you this by Express—the rider engaging to deliver it by Eight o'clock on Monday morning. The expense will be 225 dollars:—If you can collect so much to indemnify me I will thank you to do so.

I am with respect, Sir, your obedient servant,

JONATHAN GOODHUE.

We most heartily felicitate our Country on this auspicious news, which may be relied on as wholly authentic—C**entinel**.

Americans received the news of the peace treaty in February 1815.

A bronze statue of Tecumseh sits on the grounds of the United States Naval Academy in Annapolis, Maryland.

LONG-TERM EFFECTS OF THE WAR

Even though U.S. and British diplomats signed their names to the Treaty of Ghent, no document could erase the long-term effects of the fighting. The war would affect people on both sides of the Atlantic.

Effects on Native Americans

Native Americans, in particular, suffered long-term consequences. Many tribes had allied themselves with the British in the hope of preserving their lands and ways of life. In turn, Great Britain had promised Native American leaders, such as Tecumseh, that it would help them do just that once the United States was defeated. The British also promised their Native American allies help in reclaiming territories that had already been taken in U.S. expansion.

But as peace negotiations went on in the Netherlands, these promises were eventually brushed aside. The British diplomats were more concerned about ending the war than helping the Native Americans. They therefore did not protest much when U.S. diplomats objected to upholding Native American land rights. The British had wanted

Betrayal

Most of the Native Americans who had been allies with Great Britain felt greatly betrayed by the terms of the Treaty of Ghent. Black Hawk, chief of the Sauk tribe, was reported to have wept openly after discovering how poorly the interests of his people had been represented. For their part, however, many Native Americans were determined to continue to struggle to maintain their lands and ways of life. As Black Hawk pledged, "I have fought the Big Knives [white Americans] and will continue to fight them, until they retire from our lands."[1]

In 1832, Black Hawk and his followers tried to fulfill this pledge by returning to land in Illinois that had been taken from them. When they refused to leave, state troops were ordered to drive them out. The Black Hawk War (1832) resulted in the defeat and removal of the chief and his followers.

land between the United States and Canada to serve as both a buffer zone and a place for Native Americans to live undisturbed.

In addition, U.S. citizens were generally distrustful of Native Americans in the years immediately following the War of 1812. They recalled how certain tribes had supported the British during the conflict, and they worried the tribes might attack again.

As time passed, these concerns proved unfounded. Throughout the 1800s, it became clear that the North American native peoples actually had much to fear from U.S. leaders. Many politicians supported efforts to force the Native Americans westward and off land settlers wanted to occupy. One of those politicians was Andrew Jackson, who would become president in 1829. Some Native Americans resisted being pushed off their homelands, resulting in renewed conflict with the U.S. government.

Defending Canadian Territories

After the War of 1812, British leaders were not confident they could hold onto their North American territories if a similar conflict erupted in the future. As one British admiral wrote in 1817, "We cannot keep Canada if the Americans declare war against us [again]."[2]

But by the end of the 1800s, most tribes had lost most of the land that had once been theirs.

ENEMIES TURNED ALLIES

In the years following the war, the relationship between Great Britain and the United States actually improved. To date, neither nation has ever formally battled the other again. In fact, both have served together as allies during large-scale conflicts, such as World War I (1914–1918) and World War II (1939–1945).

A War Hero Worthy of Praise?

Among the heroes glorified by the War of 1812 was General Jackson. He used his successes in battle to further his career as a politician. Extremely popular with the American people, Jackson won the presidential election of 1828. Yet, while he was in control of the White House, not everyone regarded him as worthy of praise.

During and after Jackson's presidency, life for Native Americans became even more difficult. Having grown up on the frontier, the former general was determined to see the United States expand, no matter at whose expense. He was especially eager to relocate a number of Native American tribes west of the Mississippi River. He wanted U.S. citizens to claim these lands, which were rich in gold.

Although Jackson left office in 1837, his so-called Indian removal policy remained in place. Between 1838 and 1839, approximately 15,000 members of the Cherokee tribe were forced to march from their homelands in the southeastern United States to territory set aside in what is present-day Oklahoma. During the winter march, some 4,000 Cherokees died of starvation and exposure. This tragic event is frequently referred to as the Trail of Tears. By the mid-1800s, more than 45,000 Native Americans from more than a dozen tribes had been moved to reservations west of the Mississippi.

After the War of 1812, the United States and Great Britain never again fought each other in a large-scale military conflict. Nonetheless, tensions still occurred between the two nations.

One particular incident occurred during the American Civil War (1861–1865). Union officials insisted on boarding a British ship to search for and arrest Confederate diplomats on their way to England. The British, however, hoped to remain neutral during the U.S. conflict. They therefore insisted that the Union officials release and apologize to the Confederate statesmen. In the hope of avoiding another war, U.S. leaders granted the British request.

After the Treaty of Ghent, the Americans and the British immediately resumed overseas trade. In addition, Great Britain's impressments of U.S. sailors, which had been a major issue before the war, were no longer a problem. Following Napoléon Bonaparte's defeat in Europe, the British no longer had to provide a steady supply of soldiers and seamen to battle French forces.

Newfound Respect

Another positive outcome of the War of 1812 was that it made Great Britain view its former colonies with greater respect. U.S. sailors had overcome several powerful British warships during the conflict. The Americans had beaten back the British, sometimes against terrible odds, from strongholds such as Baltimore Harbor and New Orleans.

In the late 1700s and early 1800s, the United States was a young

Napoléon Bonaparte was defeated at the Battle of Waterloo near Brussels in present-day Belgium.

country that had much to prove. Great Britain, on the other hand, claimed a history that dated back centuries. During the course of the war, leaders around the world realized the United States should

be taken seriously. As noted by
one nineteenth-century British
sergeant, "War was a new game to
the Americans. But I can assure you
they improved by experience and
before peace was concluded begun
to be a formidable enemy."[3] The
Americans had waged a fierce battle
to demonstrate their independence.
And no matter whether they actually
won the overall conflict, most
historians agree that they at least
succeeded in achieving this goal.

FEELING AND ACTING MORE AS A NATION

"The war has renewed and
reinstated the national feelings and
character which the Revolution
had given, and which were daily
lessened," observed U.S. statesman
Albert Gallatin in 1816. "The people
. . . are more American; they feel
and act more as a nation; and I
hope the permanency of the Union

Historical Significance

The War of 1812 has special significance in U.S. history because it represents a second battle for national independence. Many historians argue, however, that the conflict is not as important in Great Britain's history.

One reason is the fact that the French Revolution and the Napoleonic Wars occurred at about the same time and had a greater effect on day-to-day life in Europe. In addition, much of the fighting during the War of 1812 occurred on North American soil. This meant that news of the war did not reach Great Britain until after some time, likely lessening its impact.

U.S. Congressman Albert Gallatin helped negotiate the end of the War of 1812.

is thereby better secured."[4] Gallatin was one of the diplomats who represented the United States during negotiations at Ghent. He was also one of countless Americans who believed the War of 1812 had helped shape the nation's identity.

The Americans who supported the United States during the War of 1812 could not always brag that their troops overpowered the British troops in combat. Likewise, the Americans could not boast that they had always known they would win the war or even whether it should have been fought in the first place. Yet, the Americans could proudly proclaim that they valued their independence and were eager to see their country grow and earn international respect. Despite all the bloodshed, destruction, and controversy, the War of 1812 taught Americans a priceless lesson about who they were and who they could become. ⸺

Events during the War of 1812, including the writing of "The Star-Spangled Banner," promoted unity and patriotism in the United States.

TIMELINE

1807	1807	1811
In December, Congress passes the Embargo Act of 1807; all trade with Europe is temporarily reopened 14 months later.	On June 22, the HMS *Leopard* opens fire on the USS *Chesapeake*; the British arrest four U.S. sailors.	On November 7, the Battle of Tippecanoe results in a U.S. victory over Native Americans in what is now Lafayette, Indiana.

1812	1812	1813
On October 13, U.S. forces lose the Battle of Queenston Heights in what is now Ontario, Canada.	On October 25, the USS *United States* triumphs over the HMS *Macedonian* in the eastern Atlantic.	In April, U.S. forces take control of Lake Ontario and proceed to loot and burn the Canadian settlement of York.

1812

On June 16, Lord Castlereagh announces the British will temporarily suspend all naval blockades of France and its allies.

1812

The United States formally declares war on Great Britain on June 18.

1812

On August 16, William Hull surrenders Fort Detroit to the British.

1813

On June 1, Great Britain defeats the United States in a fight between the USS *Chesapeake* and the HMS *Shannon*.

1813

On September 10, Oliver Hazard Perry captures Lake Erie from the British.

1813

On October 5, Americans triumph at the Battle of the Thames; Shawnee leader Tecumseh is killed during combat.

TIMELINE

1813

In December, the British claim a victory over U.S. troops along the Niagara frontier and then proceed to burn and loot nearby towns.

1814

In spring, French emperor Napoléon Bonaparte falls from power, allowing the British to devote more resources to the War of 1812.

1814

On July 5, U.S. troops win the Battle of Chippewa.

1814

On September 11, the U.S. Navy defeats a British invasion from Canada in the Battle of Lake Champlain.

1814

On September 13, the British launch an unsuccessful invasion of Baltimore Harbor.

1814

On December 24, the Treaty of Ghent is signed, ending the war.

1814

On July 25, both sides suffer heavy losses during the Battle of Lundy's Lane near Niagara Falls.

1814

In August, British and U.S. officials meet in Ghent, the Netherlands, to negotiate a treaty that will end the war.

1814

On August 24, the British march into Washington DC and burn down the White House and several other government buildings.

1814 –1815

From December to January, Federalist Party members meet in Connecticut for what becomes known as the Hartford Convention.

1815

On January 8, Andrew Jackson-led U.S. forces defeat the British in the Battle of New Orleans.

1815

On February 11, the HMS *Favorite* docks in the harbor outside New York City, bringing news of the Treaty of Ghent.

ESSENTIAL FACTS

DATE OF EVENT

June 18, 1812–February 18, 1815

PLACE OF EVENT

Battles in the War of 1812 took place in North America around the Canadian frontier, near and on the Great Lakes, throughout the Old Northwest territory, on and along the Atlantic, along the Gulf Coast, and in the southeast. Some battles occurred in other parts of the world, including the waters off African and South American coasts.

KEY PLAYERS

- James Madison
- Henry Clay
- Andrew Jackson
- William Henry Harrison
- Oliver Hazard Perry
- Tecumseh
- George Prevost
- Isaac Brock

HIGHLIGHTS OF EVENT

- Soon after declaring war on Great Britain in the summer of 1812, U.S. troops suffered significant defeats in the Old Northwest territory and failed in their attempt to invade Canada.
- In September 1813, U.S. Commander Oliver Hazard Perry won a fierce battle that allowed him to capture Lake Erie.

* In October 1813, the Battle of the Thames at Moraviantown resulted in a U.S. victory as well as the death of Shawnee leader Tecumseh.

* In 1814, Great Britain sent additional troops to North America following its success against Napoléon Bonaparte and the French in Europe.

* In August 1814, the British marched to Washington DC and burned down the White House and other buildings. The next month, they attempted to invade Baltimore Harbor but failed.

* In September 1814, the Americans turned back a British force invading from Canada in the Battle of Lake Champlain.

* On January 8, 1815, U.S. forces led by General Andrew Jackson won the Battle of New Orleans.

* In February 1815, Americans learned that diplomats signed the Treaty of Ghent on December 24, 1814, ending the war. On February 15, 1815, President James Madison presented the terms of the agreement to Congress, which ratified it on the eighteenth, and the world officially recognized the war as being over.

QUOTE

"The war has renewed and reinstated the national feelings and character which the Revolution had given, and which were daily lessened. The people . . . are more American; they feel and act more as a nation; and I hope the permanency of the Union is thereby better secured."—*Albert Gallatin, former U.S. secretary of the Treasury and diplomat*

ADDITIONAL RESOURCES

SELECT BIBLIOGRAPHY

Heidler, David S., and Jeanne T. Heidler. *The War of 1812*. Westport, CT: Greenwood, 2002.

Hickey, Donald R. *The War of 1812: A Forgotten Conflict*. Urbana, IL: University of Illinois Press, 1989.

Mahon, John K. *The War of 1812*. New York: Da Capo, 1991.

Remini, Robert V. *The Battle of New Orleans*. New York: Penguin, 2001.

FURTHER READING

Elish, Dan. *James Madison*. New York: Marshall Cavendish, 2008.

Greenblatt, Miriam. *War of 1812*. New York: Facts on File, 2003.

Maestro, Betsy. *A New Nation: The United States, 1783–1815*. New York: HarperCollins, 2009.

Web Links

To learn more about the War of 1812, visit ABDO Publishing Company online at **www.abdopublishing.com**. Web sites about the War of 1812 are featured on our Book Links page. These links are routinely monitored and updated to provide the most current information available.

Places To Visit

Erie Maritime Museum
150 East Front Street, Erie, PA 16507
814-452-2744
www.eriemaritimemuseum.org
This museum features a replica of the USS *Niagara* and provides extensive information about the Battle of Lake Erie.

Fort McHenry National Monument and Historic Site
2400 East Fort Avenue, Baltimore, MD 21230-5393
410-962-4290
www.nps.gov/fomc/index.htm
This historic site gives visitors a firsthand glimpse of the fort the British attacked unsuccessfully in September 1814.

The USS Constitution Museum
Charlestown Navy Yard, Building 22, Charlestown, MA 02129
617-426-1812
www.ussconstitutionmuseum.org
This museum offers tours of the historic ship and has numerous exhibits related to the War of 1812 and nineteenth-century U.S. sailors.

GLOSSARY

allies
Nations that support one another during a war.

ambassador
Someone who acts as a country's official representative in dealing with another nation.

anthem
A song or hymn that expresses admiration or gladness.

bayous
Swampy, slow-moving bodies of water.

blockade
Isolation of an area, such as a city or a harbor, by a hostile force to prevent the entry and exit of supplies and troops.

casualties
Individuals listed as wounded, missing, or dead as a result of armed conflict.

commerce
Trade in goods and services.

diplomat
An official who represents one nation in its negotiations with other nations.

embargo
A government order that makes trade with another nation illegal.

frigates
Medium-sized warships that were especially popular during the 1700s and 1800s.

impress
To force, or draft, someone into government or military service.

loot
To steal or take goods by force in a war, a riot, or a natural disaster.

martial law
Temporary rule by military officials over the civilian population during a time of national crisis, such as war.

militia
A group of civilians who are trained as soldiers but are not full-time members of a regular army.

negotiations
Discussions carried out with the goal of reaching an agreement.

neutral
Not taking either side in a conflict.

Northwest Territory
A territory, later referred to as the Old Northwest, that was organized by the United States in the 1780s and made up of land northwest of the Ohio River; it included portions of what are now the states of Ohio, Indiana, Illinois, Michigan, Wisconsin, and Minnesota.

regular
Referring to those members of a country's armed forces who are professional soldiers.

reparations
Payments designed to make up for causing damage or harm, as in a war.

strategy
A plan of action.

subjects
People who owe their loyalty to a particular nation and its leaders.

treaty
A written agreement between two or more nations that is often created for the purpose of achieving peace.

War Hawks
A group of congressmen who were eager for and encouraged a formal war with Great Britain in the early 1800s.

SOURCE NOTES

Chapter 1. The Flag That Waved On

1. "The War of 1812: American Independence Confirmed."
NPS.gov. 24 Dec. 2003. 7 Sept. 2009 <http://www.nps.gov/revwar/
unfinished_revolution/war_of_1812.html>.
2. "Real American Stories: One Nation United—'The Star-
Spangled Banner.'" *RealAmericanStories.com*. 7 Sept. 2009 <http://
www.realamericanstories.com/heritage/>.
3. "The Star-Spangled Banner: The Lyrics." *NMAH.edu*. 7 Sept.
2009 <http://americanhistory.si.edu/starspangledbanner/the-
lyrics.aspx>.

Chapter 2. The Road to War

1. "The *Chesapeake* and the *Leopard*." *TeachingAmericanHistory.org*.
8 Sept. 2009 <http://teachingamericanhistory.org/library/index.
asp?document=624>.

Chapter 3. Mixed Feelings about Fighting

1. "Letter in Support of the War of 1812." *TeachingAmericanHistory.org*.
9 Sept. 2009 <http://teachingamericanhistory.org/library/index.
asp?document=485>.
2. John C. Calhoun and H. Lee Cheek, Jr. ed. *John C. Calhoun,
Selected Writings and Speeches*. Washington DC, 2003. 227.
3. Donald R. Hickey. *The War of 1812: A Forgotten Conflict*. Urbana, IL:
University of Illinois Press, 1989. 1.
4. "An Address to the People of the Eastern States."
TeachingAmericanHistory.org. 2 Oct. 2009 <http://
teachingamericanhistory.org/library/index.asp?document=629>.

Chapter 4. Fallen Forts and Surprising Ships
1. "Save Our History: The Star-Spangled Banner Project."
History.com. 2 Oct. 2009 <http://www.history.com/starspangled_
archive/history_of_war/war14.html>.
2. David S. Heidler and Jeanne T. Heidler. *The War of 1812*.
Westport, CT: Greenwood Press, 2002. 66.
3. Donald R. Hickey. *The War of 1812: A Forgotten Conflict*. Urbana, IL:
University of Illinois Press, 1989. 97.

Chapter 5. From the Northwest to the Southeast
1. George White. *Statistics on the State of Georgia*. Savannah, GA:
W. Thorne Williams, 1849. 475.
2. David S. Heidler and Jeanne T. Heidler. *The War of 1812*.
Westport, CT: Greenwood, 2002. 78.

Chapter 6. Britain's Response to U.S. Enemies
1. "Two Accounts from the Battle of Lundy's Lane." *Galafilm.com*.
2 Oct. 2009 <http://www.galafilm.com/1812/e/events/lundy_
eyewit.html>.
2. "An Overview of the British Attack on Washington and
Baltimore." *Galafilm.com*. 2 Oct. 2009 <http://www.galafilm.
com/1812/e/events/wash.html>.
3. "The War of 1812." *OurWhiteHouse.org*. 2 Oct. 2009 <http://www.
ourwhitehouse.org/warof1812.html>.

SOURCE NOTES CONTINUED

Chapter 7. Peace Talks and Continued Combat
1. "A Description of the Hardships of the New Orleans Campaign."
Galafilm.com. 2 Oct. 2009 <http://www.galafilm.com/1812/e/people/
gleig_orl2.html>.
2. Robert V. Remini. *The Battle of New Orleans*. New York: Penguin,
2001. 43.
3. "George Gleig Describes the Aftermath of the Southern
Campaign." *Galafilm.com*. 2 Oct. 2009 <http://www.galafilm.
com/1812/e/events/orl_after.html>.
4. "Winning the Battle of New Orleans—January 8, 1815." *LOC.gov*.
2 Oct. 2009 <http://www.americaslibrary.gov/cgi-bin/page.cgi/jb/
nation/jackson_3>.

Chapter 8. Ending the Conflict
1. "Peace upon Honorable Terms." *EarlyAmerica.com*. 2 Oct. 2009
<http://www.earlyamerica.com/review/2002_winter_spring/ghent_
treaty2.htm>.
2. "Special Message to Congress on the Treaty of Ghent (February
18, 1815)." *MillerCenter.org*. 2 Oct. 2009 <http://millercenter.org/
scripps/archive/speeches/detail/3627>.
3. Ibid.
4. "Peace upon Honorable Terms." *EarlyAmerica.com*. 2 Oct. 2009
<http://www.earlyamerica.com/review/2002_winter_spring/ghent_
treaty2.htm>.

Chapter 9. Long-Term Effects of the War
1. "Black Hawk." *Galafilm.com*. 3 Oct. 2009 <http://www.galafilm.
com/1812/e/people/blackhawk.html>.
2. Barry M. Gough. *Fighting Sail on Lake Huron and Georgian Bay: The War of
1812 and Its Aftermath*. Annapolis, MD: Naval Institute, 2002. 158.
3. "Background to the Battle of Lundy's Lane." *Galafilm.com*. 3 Oct.
2009 <http://www.galafilm.com/1812/e/events/lundy.html>.
4. Albert Gallatin. *The Writings of Albert Gallatin*. Philadelphia, PA:
Lippincott, 1879. 700.

INDEX

INDEX CONTINUED

About the Author

Katie Marsico is the author of more than 50 children's books. She worked for several years as a managing editor before beginning her career as a freelance writer. She currently lives near Chicago, Illinois, with her husband, daughter, and two sons.

Photo Credits

North Wind Picture Archives, cover, 16, 20, 31, 36, 40, 56, 65, 85, 96 (top), 96 (bottom), 98, 99 (top); Getty Images, 6, 61; Bettmann/Corbis, 8; Red Line Editorial, Inc., 12, 46; Library of Congress, 15, 26, 66, 76, 83, 97, 99 (bottom); Kurtz & Allison/ Library of Congress, 25; Michael Nicholson/Corbis, 35; Kevin Fleming/Corbis, 45; Corbis, 48, 75; MPI/Getty Images, 55; AP Images, 71, 95; Time Life Pictures/Getty Images, 81; Lee Snider/ Corbis, 86; North Wind Picture Archives/AP Images, 91; Picture History, 93